# FISHING SKILLS

# Fly Tying

## Tony Whieldon

Introduction by Russ Symons

BLANDFORD

**A BLANDFORD BOOK**

This edition first published in UK
1995 by Blandford, a Cassell imprint
Wellington House, 125 Strand, London WC2R 0BB

Distributed in the United States
by Sterling Publishing Co., Inc.
387 Park Avenue South, New York, NY 10016-8810

Distributed in Australia by
Capricorn Link (Australia) Pty Ltd
2/13 Carrington Road, Castle Hill, NSW 2154

**British Library Cataloguing-in-Publication Data**
A catalogue record for this book is available from
the British Library.

ISBN 0-7137-2573-7

Printed and bound in Great Britain

# Contents

# Introduction

I am constantly amazed by the fact that such noble fish as the trout and salmon can be caught on the unlikely creations of fur and feather that we fishermen cobble together and call a fly – whether it be an imitation of some natural insect, or a flashy fly that arouses the fish's predatory instinct. Such is the enjoyment found in tying and fishing the fly that often the angler becomes as firmly hooked on the sport as the fish on the fly.

True success as an angler cannot be bought, and this applies in particular to the business of becoming a successful fly fisherman. The most expensive and perfect fly rod in the whole world cannot cover up deficiencies in a person's casting technique. A wallet of the most perfectly tied flies will assure some degree of success, if properly fished, but most fly patterns will have a regional or seasonal variation, often of a most subtle kind.

Such variations are the result of evolution, and by an intelligent response to conditions peculiar to a particular fishery or environment. The only way the fisherman can obtain flies that are in perfect accord with both his own observations of these variations, and his subjective preferences, is to tie them himself.

Tony Whieldon has drawn this book almost, it could be said, from the heart. His first love is of flyfishing, and his strongly-held view that no one can consider himself/herself a flyfisher until an apprenticeship at a fly-tying vice has been served, shines from every page.

It is through his artist's eye and interpretation – his observation of detail and the almost simplistic representation of insect life which he creates at his vice – that his skill at recognizing those features which a fish expects to occur in nature, becomes obvious. This is one of the more obtuse skills of an angler, but an essential one to any who would aspire to success.

There are some who believe in the exact imitation, or as close to it as possible within the conventions of fly fishing. Their insect imitations are wonderously close to the real thing and are a marvellous demonstration of the fly-tyer's art and skill.

But there has always been another argument. All too often the water is cloudy; water has an inherent optical distortion; light and shadow and the time of day affect the appearance of objects in the water: therefore, in view of nature's infinite nuances, the exact imitation is not always the best fish-catcher.

Tony's argument is that rather than let these nuances of light and shadow defeat the object, they should be used to enhance the allure of the fly. The silhouette should be right, but not sharply defined. Where there is a shiny surface in nature, use a material which will reflect or sparkle. Colours should be representative rather than faithfully duplicated, especially as different materials may not transmit the same colour as the original (one reason, incidentally, to follow a traditional pattern material that has been found to work).

Most important of all, however – the fly should be fished in the right manner, in the right place, and at the right time. This feel for what is right – almost an extra-sensory perception possessed by some anglers as to where the fish will be and what they will be feeding on – is a perception developed through being prepared to listen to what others have to say, and through observation and an understanding of the living world around us.

This sense of accord and observation is far more important than the precise execution of a fly-tying recipe. However, natural proportion, symmetry and movement should exert their influence not only in the tying of the fly, but in its presentation to the fish.

Tony's skill as a flyfisherman is matched by his artistic ability, then blended with a round mixture of common sense and practical ability, so that this little book contains all that is really necessary to tie flies which are effective fish-catchers. Beyond this book practice will make perfect – or so we like to think.

Russell Symons,
Plymouth, Devon.

April 1986

# Tools

VICE

HACKLE PLIERS

SCISSORS

BOBBIN~HOLDER

DUBBING NEEDLE

TWEEZERS

BEESWAX

WHIP-FINISH TOOL

DUBBING SPINNER

# Fly hooks

Sproat

The classic fly hook, having a shape ideally suited to traditional wet fly patterns. Dry flies can also be tied on this design but it is best to use a sproat with an upturned eye for very small imitations. Before tying a fly to a new hook, always check that the eye has been formed correctly.

Shallow Eye Nymph

Nymphs can be tied on any standard or long shank hook, but this special design with its narrow gape and slightly angled eye lends itself admirably to most nymph dressings.

Mustad Lure

The most widely used hook for lures and streamer flies. It is also suitable for long-bodied nymph imitations such as pheasant tails and various damsel fly nymphs.

Partridge Sedge

The perfect hook for sedge pupa imitations and various other nymphs, giving a very life-like appearance. It can also be used to give the curved swimming attitude of the freshwater shrimp.

SPROAT

MUSTAD LURE

SHALLOW EYE NYMPH

PARTRIDGE SEDGE

# Materials

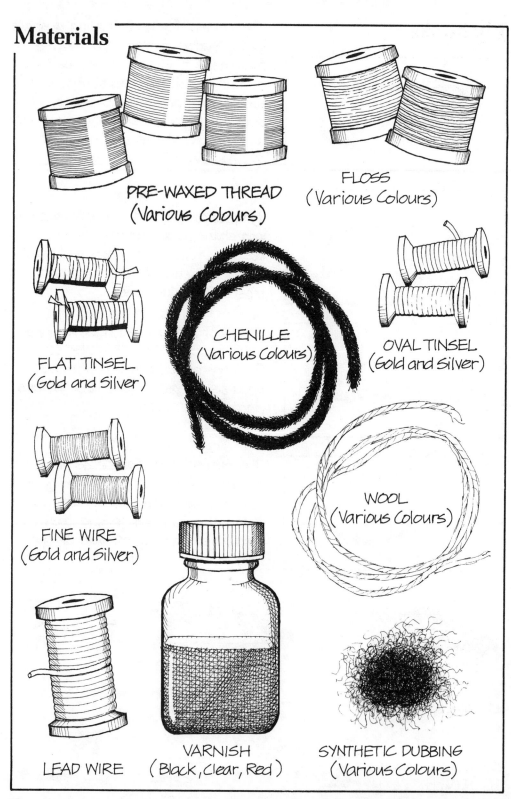

PRE-WAXED THREAD
(Various Colours)

FLOSS
(Various Colours)

FLAT TINSEL
(Gold and Silver)

CHENILLE
(Various Colours)

OVAL TINSEL
(Gold and Silver)

FINE WIRE
(Gold and Silver)

WOOL
(Various Colours)

LEAD WIRE

VARNISH
(Black, Clear, Red)

SYNTHETIC DUBBING
(Various Colours)

Peacock
Sword

Peacock
Eye Tail
Feather

Cock
Pheasant
Tail Feather

11

Jay Wing Feather

Goose Feather
Dyed Red
(Ibis Substitute)

Hen Pheasant
Wing Feather

Turkey
Tail Feather

Woodcock
Wing Feather

Mallard Drake
Wing Feather

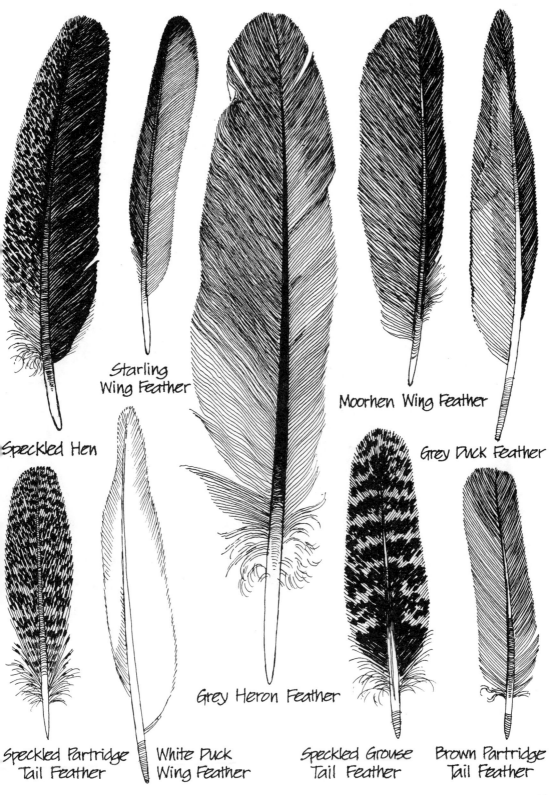

Starling
Wing Feather

Speckled Hen

Moorhen Wing Feather

Grey Duck Feather

Grey Heron Feather

Speckled Partridge
Tail Feather

White Duck
Wing Feather

Speckled Grouse
Tail Feather

Brown Partridge
Tail Feather

13

Cock hackles are best bought on the cape. The cape shown below is an actual size badger variation. The long-fibred hackles at the tip provide tail fibres for aquatic fly imitations and wings for lures (streamer flies). The middle region of the cape provides hackles for medium—size dry flies, while the small hackles at the base are ideal for dry flies tied to very small hooks. Saddle hackles, from the back of the cockerel, come individually and provide wings for large lures.

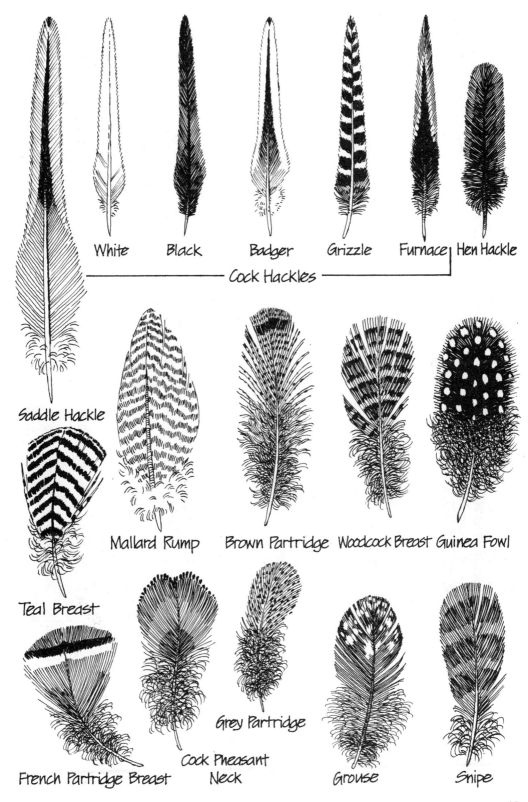

White    Black    Badger    Grizzle    Furnace   Hen Hackle

Cock Hackles

Saddle Hackle

Mallard Rump    Brown Partridge   Woodcock Breast   Guinea Fowl

Teal Breast

Grey Partridge

French Partridge Breast    Cock Pheasant Neck    Grouse    Snipe

15

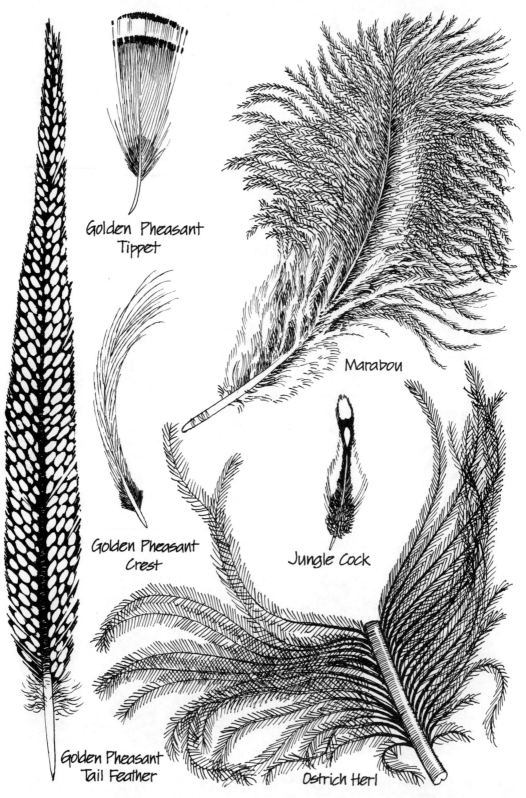

Golden Pheasant
Tippet

Marabou

Golden Pheasant
Crest

Jungle Cock

Golden Pheasant
Tail Feather

Ostrich Herl

Stoat Tail

Black Squirrel Tail          Grey Squirrel Tail          Hare's Ear

Rabbit fur

Mole fur

Deer hair

Goat hair

Seal fur

Dyed bucktail

# Workbench layout

A good light source is essential for efficient fly-tying. The vice should be situated close to a window for daytime use, but for tying after dark a lamp fitted with a daylight simulation bulb will provide the ideal illumination.

A sheet of white paper or card, positioned in front of the vice, will give a clear cut image of the fly.

Material Stock

Materials in Use

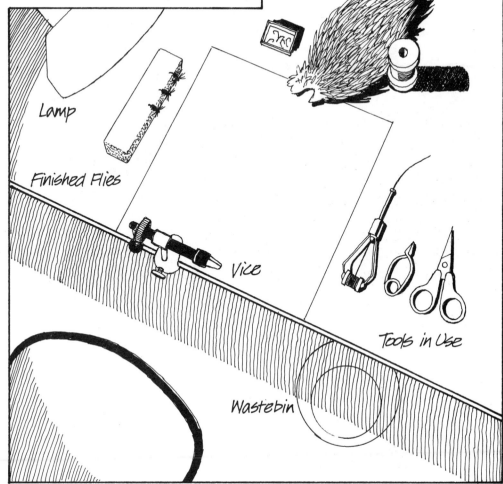

Lamp

Finished Flies

Vice

Tools in Use

Wastebin

# EPHEMEROPTERA (Mayflies)

# The trout's diet

Members of this group of insects all have upright wings and two or three tails. There are four stages in the metamorphosis: egg, nymph, sub-imago and imago. Fishermen refer to the sub-imago as the 'dun', and to the imago as the 'spinner'.

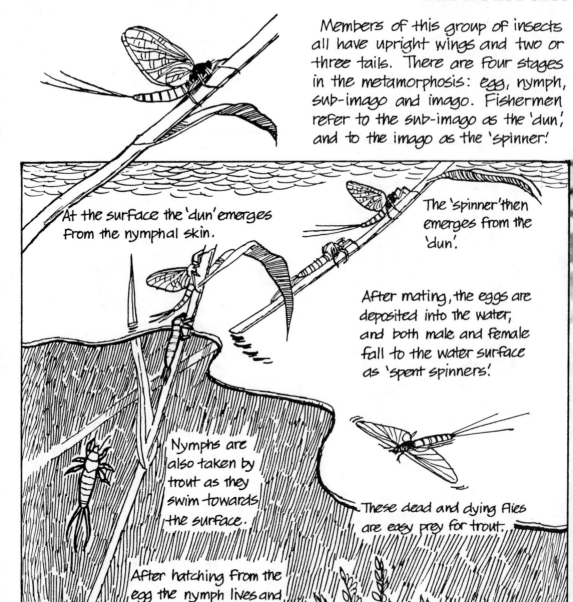

At the surface the 'dun' emerges from the nymphal skin.

The 'spinner' then emerges from the 'dun'.

After mating, the eggs are deposited into the water, and both male and female fall to the water surface as 'spent spinners'.

Nymphs are also taken by trout as they swim towards the surface.

These dead and dying flies are easy prey for trout.

After hatching from the egg the nymph lives and feeds on the bottom. Some are eaten at this stage by foraging trout.

Larva

Pupa

Adult

**CHIRONOMID MIDGE**
Also known under the name
of buzzer. The main food
item of stillwater trout.

**HAWTHORN FLY**

Larva

Adult

Pupa

**SEDGE OR CADDISFLY**

**CRANEFLY (Daddylonglegs)**

**DAMSELFLY**

Adult

**MAYFLY**

Adult    Nymph

Nymph

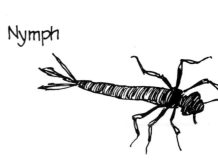

Many other species of non-aquatic insects form part of the trout's diet. These are blown on to the surface of the water by the wind. Here are the two most commonly encountered.

Crane-fly or 'daddy-long-legs'.

Hawthorn fly

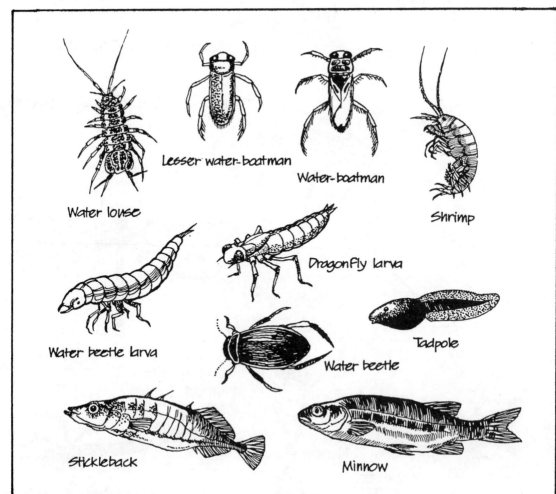

Water louse

Lesser water-boatman

Water-boatman

Shrimp

Dragonfly larva

Water beetle larva

Water beetle

Tadpole

Stickleback

Minnow

# Artificial flies

## DRY FLIES

Used when fish are taking insects from the surface of the water. Most dry flies are tied with the intention of imitating a particular species of insect.

## WET FLIES

Some of the traditional wet-fly patterns bear some resemblance to aquatic life-forms, but on the whole they are bright and flashy. The small, hackled wet flies used by the river angler for upstream fishing are, on the other hand, most lifelike.

## ANATOMY OF AN ARTIFICIAL FLY

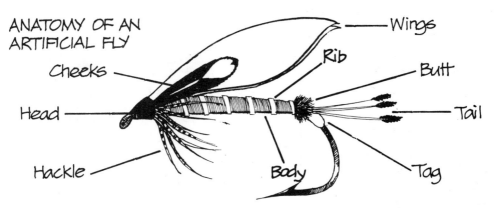

Cheeks

Head

Hackle

Rib

Body

Wings

Butt

Tail

Tag

## LURES

These probably account for more trout than all the other types combined, mainly because of their more widespread use. Colours used in their construction are as varied as the spectrum. They represent small fish rather than aquatic insects.

## NYMPHS

Patterns vary from the small buzzer pupae up to the large dragonfly nymphs. Some patterns are weighted by the inclusion of lead wire beneath the body material. Black, olive, yellow and cream are useful colours to create lifelike nymphs.

# Dubbing a body

Wind a layer of waxed thread along the shank of the hook. Apply a further rubbing of wax to the thread hanging between the hook and the bobbin.

Pinch out a small amount of dubbing and place it against the thread. Pinch the dubbing and rotate it in one direction only.

Release finger pressure and repeat the process until the dubbing is left stuck to the thread.

Dubbing Spinner

Further spinnings will eventually result in a length of dubbed silk which can be wound up the shank of the hook.

When the required length of dubbing has been wound on to the shank, any excess material left on the hanging silk can be pulled away. The rest of the fly can then be completed in the normal manner.

Where a rib material features in a dressing, which it does in most cases, the dubbing tends to flatten a little as the rib is wound over it. The dubbing can be revived by teasing the strands with a dubbing needle.

# Making a whip finish (by hand)

**7**

**8**

**9**

**10**

**11**

Final pull A

**12**

Final pull B

**13**

Final pull C

After taking
the silk over
the shank four
or five times the
whip finish will be
ready to pull tight, (Fig. 10).

# Making a whip finish (with a tool)

6

7

8

9

10

# Tying a hackled dry fly

Place a fine-wire up-eyed hook in the vice. The point of the hook should be hidden to prevent it snagging on the tying silk.

Using well-waxed tying silk, wind a neat layer along the shank of the hook. The leading end can be trapped, as shown, and the tag trimmed off before proceeding.

Select a few fibres from a cock hackle (the longer hackles in the cape are best for tails), and tie them in at the bend.

Pinch and loop the silk two or three times over the tail to clamp it to the top of the hook. One turn of silk under the tail will give it a nice cock.

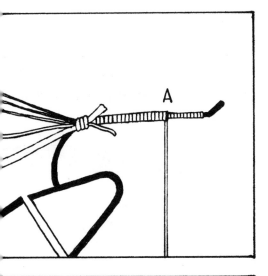

Now trap a length of body material and ribbing. Body materials vary widely, but in this instance we will assume that the fly has a body of floss silk, and a ribbing of gold wire.

After securing the components of the body, wind the silk back to the point where the body is to finish.

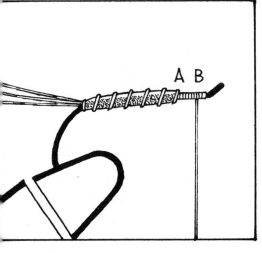

The body floss is now wound on and secured with the tying silk at point 'A'. The ribbing is then wound along the body in neat, even spirals. This also is secured with the tying silk at point 'A'. Excess body and rib material is trimmed off and the tying silk is taken to point 'B'.

Select a suitable hackle from the cape. This can best be done by bending the cape at the desired spot which will cause the hackles to stand up, making selection a lot easier. The length of the hackle fibre needs to be about one and a half times the gape of the hook.

# Tying a hackled dry fly (cont.)

Soft, fluffy fibres near the base of the hackle quill should be pulled off. The prepared hackle should now look like this.

Hold the hackle alongside the hook shank and trap the quill with two or three turns of tying silk, then pull the hackle to a position at right angles to the shank. Continue winding the tying silk, immediately behind the quill, up to the body. The hackle should now be held in a fixed position by tightly butted silk on either side. The concave bias of the hackle should face forwards.

Grip the hackle point with hackle pliers and carefully wind the hackle towards the body, where it should be trapped with two turns of silk.

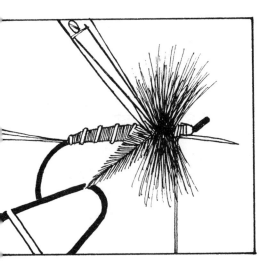

Carefully ease the tying silk back through the hackle, trapping the hackle quill in the process. Snip off the unwanted hackle tip and the excess quill. Trimming with a sharp pair of fly-tying scissors should be done with the utmost care, making sure that the points are clear of the tying silk.

Once the quill has been cut away, the head can be built up and the cut quill-end hidden from view. While this is being done it is best to hold the hackle back, out of the way.

All that remains now is to tie in a whip finish, trim off the tying silk and treat the head of the fly with a drop of clear varnish.

# Hackled dry fly dressings

## PHEASANT TAIL
Hook: 10-14
Tying silk: Brown
Body: Cock pheasant tail fibres
ribbed with gold wire
Hackle: Golden dun cock
Tail: Golden dun cock hackle
Fibres

## GREY DUSTER
Hook: 10-14
Tying silk: Brown
Body: Dubbing of light rabbit
fur mixed with a small
amount of blue underfur
Hackle: Badger cock with a
good dark centre

## COCH-Y-BONDDU
Hook: 12-14
Tying silk: Brown
Body: Two or three strands of
peacock herl with fine flat
gold tinsel tag
Hackle: Furnace cock

## TUP'S INDISPENSABLE
Hook: 14-16
Tying silk: Yellow
Body: Rear end, yellow floss or
tying silk—remainder pinkish
lambs wool
Hackle: Honey cock.
Tail: Honey cock hackle fibres

## IRON BLUE DUN
Hook: 12-14
Tying silk: Red
Body: Mole-fur dubbing with
red tying-silk butt
Hackle: Iron blue cock
Tail: Iron blue cock hackle Fibres

## BLUE UPRIGHT
Hook: 10-14
Tying silk: Purple
Body: Well marked stripped
peacock quill
Hackle: Medium blue dun cock
Tail: Blue dun cock hackle Fibres

## RED SPINNER
Hook: 12–14
Tying silk: Brown
Body: Red floss, ribbed with
fine flat gold tinsel
Hackle: Rear, Red cock—
Front, Blue dun cock
Tail: Red cock hackle fibres

## GINGER QUILL
Hook: 14–16
Tying silk: Orange
Body: Stripped peacock quill
Hackle: Ginger cock
Tail: Ginger cock hackle fibres

## MARCH BROWN
Hook: 10–14
Tying silk: Yellow
Body: Hare's fur spun thinly
Hackle: Rear, Dun cock—
Front, Brown partridge back
feather
Tail: Back feather fibres

## RED TAG
Hook: 12–14
Tying silk: Brown
Body: Bronze peacock herl
Tag: Bright red wool or floss
Hackle: Red cock

## CINNAMON QUILL
Hook: 12–14
Tying silk: Brown
Body: Stripped peacock herl
Hackle: Ginger cock
Tail: Ginger cock hackle fibres

## DOUBLE BADGER
Hook: 12–14
Tying silk: Black
Body: Three strands of
peacock herl
Hackle: Badger cock—one at
the head and one at the tail

# Tying an upright-winged dry fly

Place a fine-wire hook in the vice and proceed exactly as with a hackled dry fly up to the point where the body has been completed.

It is purely a matter of choice whether an up-eyed or down-eyed hook is used. The former looks prettier, but I doubt very much that the trout has such aesthetic discrimination.

The wings are cut from a pair of matching left and right wing feathers.

When placed together the wing slips should have the concave faces pointing outwards. Handle the slips very gingerly at this stage, as they have a tendency to break up. If this does occur, cut a new set.

To minimize the risk of this happening grip the slips firmly; try to avoid a sliding movement between finger and thumb.

Pinch the slips together between the forefinger and thumb and hold them on the hook shank. Form a long loop over the slips, between finger and thumb, and pull down to trap the wings against the hook shank. Three turns of silk should be enough to hold the slips in place. Check that the slips are sitting squarely along the hook shank.

Move the finger and thumb to the tip of the slips and lift them upright. Make a couple of turns of silk tight against the front edge of the slips to trap them in an upright position.

Take one turn of silk around the base of the wing slips.

Trim off any excess wing material.

# Tying an upright-winged dry fly (cont.)

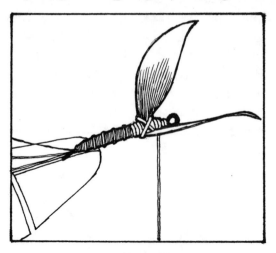

Now make a cross-over of silk between the wings, easing them apart a little more.

Select a good quality cock hackle and tie on, using the same procedure as in the tying of the hackled dry fly. Wind the hackle carefully around the shank, first in front of the wings, then to the rear. Trap the end of the hackle with tying silk and then bring the silk back through the hackle, making sure that the wings are not disfigured in the process.

Trim off the waste hackle point and quill, build up a neat head, whip finish and trim off the silk. Coat the head with clear varnish.

# Winged dry fly dressings

### COACHMAN

| | |
|---|---|
| Hook | 10-16. |
| Silk | Brown. |
| Body | Bronze peacock herl. |
| Wings | From a white duck wing. |
| Hackle | Natural red cock. |

### RED QUILL

| | |
|---|---|
| Hook | 14-16. |
| Silk | Red. |
| Body | Stripped peacock herl. |
| Wings | From a starling wing. |
| Hackle and tail | Red cock. |

### FLIGHT'S FANCY

| | |
|---|---|
| Hook | 12-16. |
| Silk | Yellow. |
| Body | Pale yellow floss, ribbed with flat gold tinsel. |
| Wings | From a pale starling wing. |
| Hackle and tail | Honeydun cock. |

### POPE'S NONDESCRIPT

| | |
|---|---|
| Hook | 12-16. |
| Silk | Crimson. |
| Body | Apple green floss, ribbed with flat gold tinsel. |
| Wings | From a starling wing. |
| Hackle and tail | Red cock. |

### HARDY'S FAVOURITE

| | |
|---|---|
| Hook | 10-14. |
| Silk | Red. |
| Body | Claret floss silk, ribbed with bronze peacock herl. |
| Wings | From a woodcock wing. |
| Hackle | Partridge breast feather. |
| Tail | Golden pheasant tippets. |

### GOLD-RIBBED HARE'S EAR

| | |
|---|---|
| Hook | 12-16. |
| Silk | Yellow. |
| Body | Dubbed hare's fur ribbed with flat gold tinsel. |
| Wings | From a pale wing feather of a starling. |
| Hackle | Longer strands of the body picked out with a needle. |

### YELLOW SALLY
Hook | 12-16.
Silk | Primrose.
Body | Yellow dyed seal's fur, ribbed with primrose tying silk.
Wings | From any fine light-coloured wing dyed yellow.
Hackle | Natural light ginger cock.

### WICKHAM'S FANCY
Hook | 12-14.
Silk | Brown.
Body | Flat gold tinsel, ribbed with fine gold wire.
Tail | Red cock fibres.
Wings | From starling or duck wing.
Hackle | Red game cock.

### ROUGH OLIVE
Hook | 12-14.
Silk | Brown.
Body | Heron herl dyed olive, ribbed with gold wire.
Wings | From a starling wing feather.
Hackle | Dark blue dun cock.

### DRIFFIELD DUN
Hook | 14-16.
Silk | Yellow.
Body | Pale blue seal's fur, ribbed with yellow tying silk.
Wings | From a pale, starling feather.
Hackle | Ginger cock.

### GREENWELL'S GLORY
Hook | 12-14.
Silk | Yellow (Well waxed).
Body | Yellow tying silk, ribbed with fine gold wire.
Wings | From a dark starling feather.
Hackle | Light furnace cock.

### HOFLAND'S FANCY
Hook | 12-16.
Silk | Yellow.
Body | Crimson floss with yellow tying silk butt.
Wings | From a hen pheasant wing.
Hackle | Natural red cock.

# Tying a variant dry fly

Tie the wings exactly as shown for the upright-wing version, but omit the turns of silk which bring the wings to the upright position as shown in Fig. 6.

Tie the complete hackle to the rear of the wings, then bring the silk to the front of the wings, whip finish and varnish.

### BADGER VARIANT

| | |
|---|---|
| Tying silk | Red. |
| Body | Stripped peacock quill. |
| Wings | From a starling wing feather. |
| Hackle | Badger cock, large. |

### RED VARIANT

| | |
|---|---|
| Tying silk | Red. |
| Body | Stripped peacock quill. |
| Wings | From a starling wing feather. |
| Hackle | Natural red cock, large. |

### RUSTY VARIANT

| | |
|---|---|
| Tying silk | Red. |
| Body | Yellow floss. |
| Wings | From a partridge wing feather. |
| Hackle | Rusty dun cock, large. |

### GREENWELL'S VARIANT

| | |
|---|---|
| Body | Waxed yellow tying silk ribbed with fine gold wire. |
| Wings | From a starling wing feather. |
| Hackle | Light furnace cock, large. |

# Tying a spent-wing dry fly

After tying the body, as described earlier, select two hackles of equal size. Strip away the fibres to leave the length of wing required. Cut away excess quill and whip both hackles to the hook shank.

Pull each hackle back separately and lock into position as shown. Take two or three turns of silk towards the eye. This is the point where the hackle will start, and the procedure for tying that is exactly as shown for the hackled and winged dry fly.

Before tying in the hackle, snip off any excess hackle quill, especially if it is overlapping the body.

# Spent-wing dry fly dressings

### LUNN'S PARTICULAR
| | |
|---|---|
| Hook | 14–16. |
| Tying silk | Crimson. |
| Tail | Natural red cock hackle fibres. |
| Body | Natural red cock hackle stalk. |
| Wings | Medium blue dun cock hackle tips. |
| Hackle | Natural medium red cock. |

### HOUGHTON RUBY
| | |
|---|---|
| Hook | 14–16. |
| Tying silk | Crimson. |
| Tail | White cock hackle fibres. |
| Body | Hackle stalk dyed red. |
| Wings | Light blue dun hen hackle tips. |
| Hackle | Bright Rhode Island Red cock. |

### WINGED YELLOW BOY
| | |
|---|---|
| Hook | 14–16. |
| Tying silk | Pale orange. |
| Tail | Pale buff hackle fibres. |
| Body | White hackle stalk dyed medium yellow. |
| Wings | Light buff cock hackle tips. |
| Hackle | Light buff cock. |

### SHERRY SPINNER
| | |
|---|---|
| Hook | 14–16 |
| Tying silk | Pale orange. |
| Tail | Pale ginger hackle fibres. |
| Body | Orange floss silk ribbed with fine gold wire. |
| Wings | Light blue dun hen hackle tips. |
| Hackle | Rhode Island Red cock. |

# Mayfly dressings

### SPENT GNAT
Tail    Three fibres from a cock pheasant tail.
Body    White translucent plastic.
Wings    Dark blue hackle points.
Hackle    Badger cock.

### YELLOW PARTRIDGE HACKLE
Tail    Three fibres from a cock pheasant tail.
Body    White floss silk.
Rear hackle    Yellow cock.
Front hackle    Grey partridge.

### HACKLE FIBRE WING
Tail    Three fibres from a cock pheasant tail.
Body    Natural raffia, ribbed with silver oval tinsel.
Body hackle    Medium olive cock.
Wings    Fibres of large honey dun cock hackle dyed olive, and tied upright.
Shoulder hackle    Badger cock dyed yellow.

### HACKLED SPENT
Tail    Three or more fibres from the rump feather of a golden pheasant.
Body    Fluorescent white floss.
Rear hackle    Black cock.
Shoulder hackle    White, grizzle or badger cock.

# Tying a Hawthorn fly

Place a size 10 or 12 down-eyed sproat hook in the vice and run tying silk from the eye to well around the bend. Tie in a length of black floss and take the silk and floss back two-thirds of the way along the shank. At this point, tie in a length of black chenille.

Just forward of the chenille, tie in two white cock hackle points.

Take the silk forward a little and wind the chenille carefully forward, around the wings, to build up a thorax.

Select a very long-fibred cock or hen hackle and tie in immediately forward of the thorax. Pull all the fibres down and trap the bases with tying silk, building up a head in the process. Whip finish and coat the head with black varnish.

# Tying a winged wet fly

Clamp a down-eyed sproat hook in the vice and run a layer of waxed tying silk along the shank.

The characteristic bend of a sproat hook can be used to good effect by taking the tying silk well into the bend, giving the body a more natural, less rigid appearance.

Select the tail material and tie it down with two or three turns of silk. Follow this with a length of ribbing, if required, and finally a length of body material. Return the tying silk back towards the eye leaving enough space to tie in the hackle and wings.

Wind the body material along the shank and tie it down. Follow this with the rib, which should be evenly spaced along the body.

I usually take a turn of ribbing around the hook shank before proceeding along the body.

Trim off excess body and ribbing material in preparation for tying in the hackle and wings.

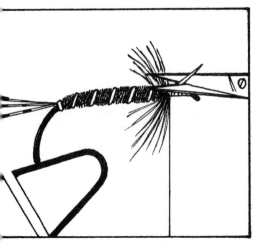

Select a hackle of the type required and tie down with the face of the feather looking forward, so that when it is wound on to the shank the fibres have a bias towards the bend of the hook. Two or three turns of hackle are ample. Tie down the hackle point and cut it away, then return the silk to the front of the hackle and trim off excess quill.

Moisten the forefinger and thumb and brush the hackle down and back. Make two or three turns of silk at the junction of the hackle and hook shank. The result should look like this.

Select two matching slips from a wing feather. Place them together so that the convex edges are facing outwards, opposite to those used on a dry fly.

# Tying a winged wet fly (cont.)

Grip the wing slips firmly between forefinger and thumb and position them on the hook shank. The point of the wings should just overlap the extreme end of the hook bend.

Clamp the wings firmly against the shank of the hook with two or three pinch and loops.

If the wings need to be lifted a little in order to improve the appearance of the fly a turn of tying silk can be taken to the rear

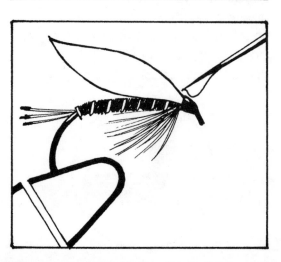

Trim away the excess wing material, build up a stream-lined head and whip finish.

Finally, using the dubbing needle, give the head a coat of varnish.

# Winged wet fly dressings

### SILVER MARCH BROWN
Tail    Fibres from partridge back feather.
Body    Flat silver tinsel, ribbed oval silver tinsel.
Hackle    Partridge back feather.
Wings    From hen pheasant wing.

### ALEXANDRA
Tail    Red ibis feather slip.
Body    Flat silver tinsel.
Hackle    Black hen.
Wings    Six to eight strands of green peacock sword herl, with a slip of red ibis each side.

### BUTCHER
Tail    Red ibis slip.
Body    Flat silver tinsel.
Hackle    Black hen.
Wings    From the blue wing-feather of a mallard drake.

### ALDER
Body    Peacock herl ribbed with claret tying silk.
Hackle    Black hen.
Wings    From a brown speckled hen's wing feather.

### PETER ROSS
Tail    Fibres from a golden pheasant tippet feather.
Body    Rear half – Flat silver tinsel. Front half – Dyed red seal's fur.
Rib    Oval silver tinsel over both halves.
Hackle    Black hen.
Wings    From the breast or flank feather of a teal.

### MALLARD & CLARET
Tail    Fibres from a golden pheasant tippet feather.
Body    Claret seal's fur.
Rib    Oval gold tinsel.
Hackle    Natural red cock.
Wings    Bronze speckled feather from a mallard shoulder.

## CONNEMARA BLACK

Tail    Golden pheasant crest feather.
Body   Black seal's fur, ribbed with Fine oval tinsel.
Hackle  Natural black cock beneath blue jay fibres.
Wings  From the bronze shoulder feather of a mallard.

## DUNKELD

Tail    Golden pheasant crest.
Body   Flat gold tinsel, ribbed with oval gold tinsel.
Hackle  Dyed orange cock tied palmer fashion.
Wings  Bronze mallard.
Cheeks  Two jungle cock feathers.

## INVICTA

Tail    Golden pheasant crest feather.
Body   Yellow seal's fur, ribbed with oval gold tinsel.
Body hackle  Ginger cock.
Head hackle  Blue jay fibres.
Wings  From a hen pheasant tail feather.

## PARMACHENE BELLE

Tail    Red and white duck feather.
Butt    Black ostrich herl.
Body   Yellow floss silk, ribbed with flat gold tinsel.
Hackle  Dyed scarlet cock and white cock.
Wings  White duck with a red ibis slip each side.

## PROFESSOR

Tail    Red ibis feather slip.
Body   Yellow floss silk, ribbed with gold tinsel.
Hackle  Natural ginger cock.
Wing  From the flank feather of a grey mallard.

## ROYAL COACHMAN

Tail    Strands from a golden pheasant tippet.
Body   Scarlet floss with a bronze peacock herl butt and thorax.
Hackle  Natural light red cock.
Wings  Slips from any white wing feather.

# Tying a Corixa (Water-boatman)

Clamp a size 12-14 down-eyed hook in the vice and run tying silk to the bend. Tie in a length of wire or oval tinsel ribbing, followed by a length of green or orange wool. Take a slip of fibres from a cock pheasant tail feather and tie at the same point, then run the silk back, almost to the eye.

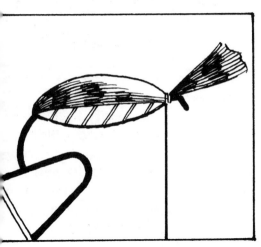

Build up a body with the wool and tie it down. Run the ribbing in neat spirals back along the body and tie it down. Trim off excess body and rib material.

Now pull the pheasant fibres right over the body, tie down and trim away excess material.

Select two long fibres from a cock pheasant tail and tie on at each side of the head. The thicker ends of the fibres should point to the rear. Build up a large head and treat it with a coat of clear varnish. A layer of clear varnish over the back is also advisable.

Top view

# Tying a hackled wet fly

Hackles used for this type of fly need to be soft. Partridge, hen, snipe or woodcock are ideal.

When fished in running water the fibres of these hackles move in the current, giving the fly a most life like appearance.

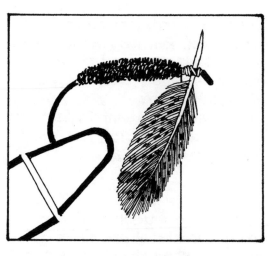

Place a down-eyed size 14-10 hook in the vice and tie in a body.

Select a good quality hackle and tether it to the hook shank with the face of the feather pointing forward. Hold the tip of the hackle with hackle pliers and make just two or three turns around the shank.

Trim off excess hackle tip and quill, build up a neat head and coat it with clear varnish.

Hackle before       Hackle ready
preparation         to be tied

# Hackled wet fly dressings

### PARTRIDGE & ORANGE
Body   Bright orange floss or silk.
Hackle  Brown partridge back feather.

### BROWN SPIDER
Body   Bronze peacock herl.
Hackle  Brown partridge back feather.

### SNIPE & PURPLE
Body   Purple floss.
Hackle  Small feather from snipe's wing.

### BRACKEN CLOCK
Body   Bronze peacock herl and red silk.
Hackle  Cock pheasant neck feather.

### BLACK SPIDER
Body   Black tying silk or floss.
Hackle  Black hen hackle.

### WATERHEN BLOA
Body   Mole fur spun on yellow silk.
Hackle  Feather from underside of moorhen's wing.

### BLACK & PEACOCK SPIDER
Body   Three strands of peacock herl over black floss underbody.
Hackle  Black hen hackle.

### GROUSE & YELLOW
Body   Yellow floss silk ribbed with fine gold wire.
Hackle  Grouse breast feather.

# Tying a palmer

Run the tying silk from the eye to the bend of the hook and tie in a length of wire or tinsel. Tie in a length of body material and wind the silk back to a position just short of the eye. Wind the body material to this point, tie down and trim away any excess. Prepare and tie in a hackle against the front of the body.

Grip the hackle point in a pair of hackle pliers and take the hackle, around the body, to the bend of the hook. Now, very carefully but firmly, wind the ribbing back through the hackle and tie it down with the silk. The ribbing is now holding the hackle stem secure all along the body.

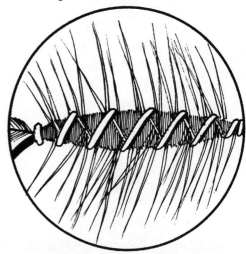

Remove the hackle pliers and trim away the hackle point, excess quill and ribbing material.

An extra hackle can now be tied at the front, if required. In my opinion this improves the appearance of the Fly and helps to provide extra buoyancy if it is being used as a floating pattern.

On predominantly dark patterns a white forward hackle aids visibility when the fly is being fished in shadow beneath overhanging foliage.

## Palmer dressings

### BROWN PALMER
Body    Brown wool or seal's fur.
Rib     Gold wire or oval gold tinsel.
Hackle  Brown cock.

### STEEL BLUE
Body    Peacock herl with orange tag.
Rib     Gold wire.
Hackle  Grizzle cock.

### ZULU
Tail    Red ibis feather or red wool.
Body    Black wool or seal's fur.
Rib     Flat silver tinsel.
Hackle  Black cock.

### ARTFUL DODGER
Body    Purple wool.
Rib     Gold wire.
Wings   From a cock pheasant's wing.
Hackle  Red cock.

# Tying a nymph

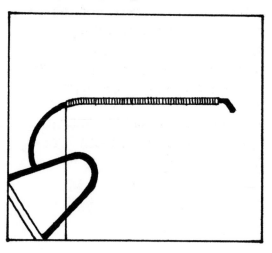

Place a long-shanked hook in the vice and run tying silk from the eye to the bend.

Tie in the tail material, if needed, followed by the ribbing and the body material.

In this instance we will assume that the body is made of seal's fur, which has to be dubbed on to the tying silk prior to being wound along the hook shank. ( See section on dubbing a body).

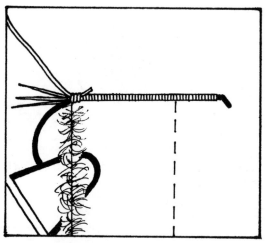

Take the dubbed silk, in turns, about two-thirds of the way back along the hook shank. Remove any excess dubbing from the hanging silk. Now carefully wind the rib material along the body and tie it down. A slip of feather fibres is now tied in by one end, which eventually forms the wing cases.

More seal's fur is now dubbed on to the silk in preparation for forming the thorax. This is usually a different colour to the main body. Remember not to overdo the dubbing as this will result in a bulky mess.

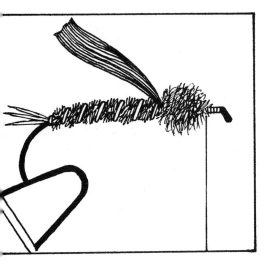

Wind the dubbed silk towards the eye of the hook. Stop just short of the eye, leaving enough space to tie in the hackle and form the head.

The hackle is tied in exactly the same way as that of a hackled wet fly. Trim away any excess hackle quill.

Now grip the end of the feather fibres and pull them over the thorax and the hackle. Tie down with a few turns of silk and trim away any excess material. Build a neat head, whip finish, trim off silk and varnish.

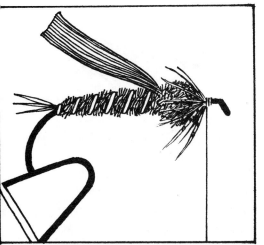

Some patterns of nymph have wing cases over the body or over the body and thorax.

Wing cases tied in at the bend of the hook and pulled over before the thorax is dubbed.

Wing cases tied in at the bend of the hook and pulled over before the head is formed.

# Nymph dressings

## SEDGE PUPA (JOHN GODDARD)
Body | Orange seal's fur.
Rib | Oval silver tinsel.
Thorax | Dark brown condor herl.
Wing cases | Pale brown condor herl.
Hackle | Honey hen, tied sparsely.

## MAYFLY NYMPH
Tail | Three strands from a cock pheasant's tail feather.
Body | Natural seal's fur.
Thorax | Brown olive seal's fur.
Rib | Oval gold tinsel.
Wing cases | From a hen pheasant tail.
Hackle | Brown partridge.

## AMBER NYMPH
Body | Amber yellow seal's fur.
Thorax | Dark brown or orange seal's fur.
Wing cases | Fibres of any brownish feather tied over the body.
Hackle | Honey hen hackle fibres.

## PAMSELFLY NYMPH
Tail | Three olive green hackle points.
Body | Olive seal's fur.
Rib | Flat gold tinsel.
Thorax | Dark olive seal's fur.
Wing cases | Fibres from a brown mallard shoulder feather.
Hackle | Grouse hackle fibres.

## MONTANA STONE
Body | Black chenille.
Thorax | Yellow or orange chenille.
Wing cases | Black chenille.
Hackle | Black hen.

## IVEN'S GREEN & BROWN NYMPH
Tail | Three strands of peacock herl.
Body | Olive green ostrich herl.
Wing cases | Peacock herl.
Thorax | Peacock herl.

# Tying a Midge Pupa (Buzzer)

There are many variations on this imitation and, no doubt, they all take their share of trout if fished correctly. My variation is no exception and is simplicity itself to tie.

Place a size 16–10 Yorkshire caddis hook in the vice and run well waxed tying silk from the eye to well around the bend. Tie in a plume made from a short length of fluorescent white floss. A tap with the finger on the end of the floss will open it out.

Tie in a length of brown, black or green floss and take the tying silk back to point A. Wind on the floss body and tie down.

Tie in two or three lengths of fluorescent white floss and wind the silk to point B. Wind the strands of white floss, together, to point B, and tie down. Whip finish and varnish.

The plume at the front may have to be trimmed, and a few taps with the finger will open out the fibres to give a natural appearance.

# Tying a lure (hackle-winged)

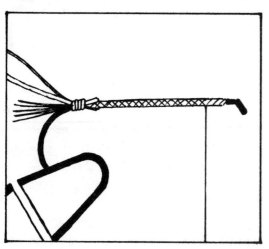

Clamp a down-eyed long-shanked hook in the vice and run well-waxed silk, in open turns, up to the bend. Tie in the tail, if needed, followed by the ribbing and the body material and run the silk back just short of the eye.

Wind the body material back to the hanging silk and tie it down. Do the same with the rib, making sure that it is evenly spaced all the way along the body. Trim off excess material.

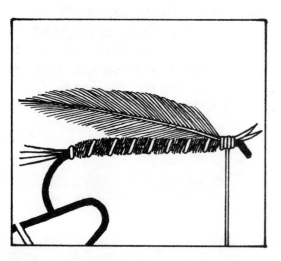

Select two long, good quality cock hackles and hold them, back-to-back, between forefinger and thumb along the top of the body. The hackle points should extend just beyond the bend of the hook. Using the pinch and loop method, tie them down with three or four turns of silk.

Owing to their scarcity and price jungle cock feathers are not used as often as they once were. However, there are signs that they will once again be readily available in the not-too-distant future, as the bird is being reared in captivity by a few enterprising and imaginative breeders. If you do possess any of these striking feathers now is the point at which to tie them in, on each side of the wings. Check to see that they are positioned nicely before proceeding any further.

Turn the hook over in the vice. Pull off a bunch of fibres from a cock hackle, and using the pinch and loop method secure them with two or three turns of silk. Before tying them down completely, rub across the fibres with the thumb nail to spread them a little.

Build up a sleek-looking head and whip finish. Coat the head with red or black varnish. An eye decoration can be painted on if jungle cock is not being used.

# Tying a lure (hair-winged)

Place a long-shanked down-eyed hook in the vice and run well-waxed tying silk down to the bend. Using the required materials, make the body in the usual manner.

Cut a bunch of hairs of the required variety and lay it along the top of the hook shank. The tips of the hairs should extend just beyond the bend of the hook.

Take three or four turns of silk around the hairs and hook-shank using the pinch-and-loop procedure.

 Half hitch

To prevent the fibres coming adrift during use, apply a blob of clear varnish which will be sucked into the wing by the capillary action of the hairs. Take a few more turns of silk around the hairs and make a half hitch.

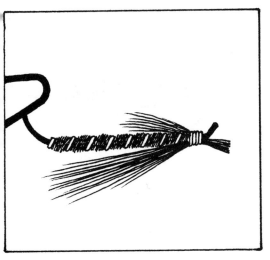

Turn the fly over in the vice and tie on a beard hackle in exactly the same way as for the hackle-winged lure, and trim off any excess hackle.

Turn the fly upright again and trim off any excess wing material.

When trimming off excess wing material, cut at an angle, in order to produce a neater head.

An additional embellishment for hackle or hairwing lures can be made by cutting a section of ball chain and tying this, in the manner shown, to produce a bug-eyed look.

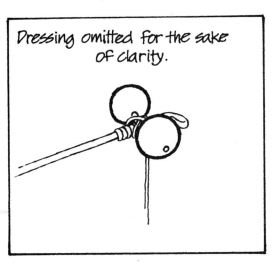

Dressing omitted for the sake of clarity.

# Lure dressings

### MISSIONARY
| | |
|---|---|
| Tail | Scarlet-dyed cock hackle Fibres. |
| Body | White chenille. |
| Rib | Silver tinsel. |
| Wing | Whole mallard breast feather. |
| Hackle | Scarlet-dyed cock hackle Fibres. |

### JERSEY HERD
| | |
|---|---|
| Tail and Back | Fibres of bronze peacock herl. |
| Body | Shaped with silk and covered with gold tinsel. |
| Hackle | Hot orange cock. |
| Head | Two or three turns of peacock herl. |

### BADGER LURE
| | |
|---|---|
| Body | Fluorescent orange wool. |
| Rib | Oval silver tinsel. |
| Wing | Two large badger cock hackles. |
| Hackle | Hot orange cock hackle Fibres. |
| Eyes | Two jungle cock Feathers. |

### VIVA
| | |
|---|---|
| Tag | Lime green fluorescent wool. |
| Body | Black chenille. |
| Rib | Flat silver tinsel. |
| Wing | Black marabou fibres. |
| Hackle | Black cock hackle fibres. |

### ACE OF SPADES
| | |
|---|---|
| Body | Black chenille. |
| Rib | Oval silver tinsel. |
| Wing | Black hen hackle tied matuka fashion. |
| Overwing | Bronze mallard. |
| Hackle | Guinea fowl fibres. |

### RED & BLACK MATUKA
| | |
|---|---|
| Body | Red chenille. |
| Rib | Oval gold tinsel. |
| Wing | Two black hen hackles tied matuka fashion. |
| Eyes | Jungle cock feathers. |
| Hackle | Black cock hackle fibres. |

### SWEENEY TODD

| | |
|---|---|
| Body | Rear – Black floss silk.<br>Front – DFM magenta floss. |
| Rib | Silver tinsel or Lurex. |
| Hackle | Crimson cock. |
| Wing | Black squirrel tail hair. |

### JACK FROST

| | |
|---|---|
| Tag | Crimson wool. |
| Body | White wool. |
| Hackles | Crimson cock followed by white cock. |
| Wing | White marabou. |

### CHURCH FRY

| | |
|---|---|
| Tail | Bunch of white hackle fibres. |
| Body | Orange chenille. |
| Rib | Gold or silver tinsel. |
| Hackle | Crimson. |
| Wing | Natural grey squirrel tail hair. |

### BLACK LURE
#### (Often tied tandem fashion)

| | |
|---|---|
| Body | Black chenille or floss. |
| Rib | Silver tinsel. |
| Hackle | Black cock fibres. |
| Wing | Four black cock hackles. |

### WHISKY FLY

| | |
|---|---|
| Silk | Orange |
| Tag | DFM scarlet nylon floss. |
| Body | Wide silver tinsel or Lurex. |
| Rib | DFM scarlet nylon floss. |
| Hackle | Hot orange cock. |
| Wing | Hot orange calf's tail hair. |

### BLACK GHOST

| | |
|---|---|
| Tail | Golden pheasant crest. |
| Body | Black wool or floss. |
| Rib | Flat silver tinsel. |
| Hackle | Golden pheasant crest. |
| Wing | White cock hackles. |
| Cheeks | Jungle cock. |

# Tying a tandem lure

Tandem lures can be tied on long-shank or standard hooks. Cut a length of heavy nylon monofilament line and whip it to two hooks with heavy tying silk. Form a couple of simple hitch knots on the nylon line to prevent it slipping under the whipping. Reinforce this with a coat of clear varnish and allow to dry.

The example shown here is a worm fly, a long-established lure with many large trout to its credit.

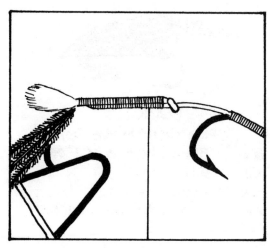

Put the rear hook in the vice first and run the tying silk to the bend of the hook. Tie in a tail of red wool and a few fibres of peacock herl. Take the tying silk back, almost to the eye, and wind the body material to the same point and tie it down with silk.

Trim off any excess body herl and tie in a natural dark red hen or cock hackle to slope well back over the body. Whip finish and coat the head with black varnish.

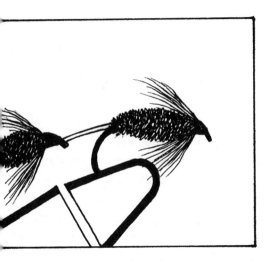

The front hook is then put in the vice and tied in exactly the same manner as the rear hook. The tail, however, is omitted.

Long-shank hook tandem lures have only the body material tied to the rear hook.

## Tandem lure dressings

### BADGER LURE

| | |
|---|---|
| Silk | Orange. |
| Bodies | Fluorescent orange wool. |
| Rib | Oval silver tinsel. |
| Hackle | Hot orange cock. |
| Wing | Two large badger hackles. |
| Eyes | Two jungle cock feathers. |

### BLACK LURE

| | |
|---|---|
| Silk | Black. |
| Bodies | Black floss or chenille. |
| Rib | Oval silver tinsel. |
| Hackle | Black cock fibres. |
| Wing | Two or four long, black cock hackles. |

### SWEENEY TODD TANDEM

| | |
|---|---|
| Silk | Black. |
| Bodies | Black floss silk. |
| Rib | Oval silver tinsel. |
| Throat | Magenta fluorescent wool. |
| Hackle | Crimson cock hackle fibres. |
| Wing | Black squirrel tail fibres. |

### CHURCH FRY TANDEM

| | |
|---|---|
| Silk | Brown. |
| Bodies | Orange floss silk. |
| Rib | Flat silver tinsel or Lurex. |
| Throat | Magenta fluorescent wool. |
| Hackle | Orange cock hackle fibres. |
| Wing | Grey squirrel tail fibres. |

# Tying a Muddler Minnow

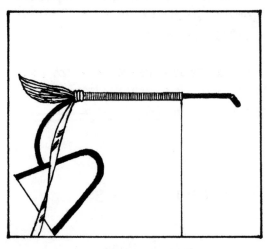

Wind black or brown tying silk from a point half way along the shank of a long-shanked hook to the bend. Tie in a slip of turkey wing for the tail and a length of flat gold tinsel, then return the silk to its starting point. Wind the gold tinsel to form a body, and tie it down.

A bunch of grey squirrel tail hair is then tied to the shank to extend well beyond the bend of the hook.

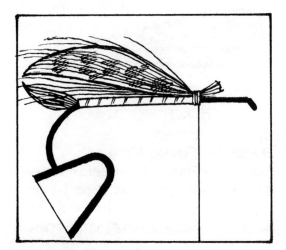

Two sections of mottled (oak) turkey feather are then tied over the squirrel hair, again extending past the bend of the hook. Make a half-hitch at this point in preparation for spinning the deer hair along the bare hook shank.

Cut a bunch of deer hair and grip it tightly to prevent the hairs sliding out of place.

Hold the hairs along the top of the hook shank with the cut ends pointing forward.

Take two loose turns of silk over the hairs.

Pull down tight on the silk, and at the same time rotate the finger and thumb in the same direction as the turning deer hair. The first spinning should look like this.

Take the silk to the front of the hairs and form a hitch, in readiness for the next spinning.

After each spinning the hairs will have to be pushed back. This is best done with an empty ball pen casing or something similar.

After a few spinnings the head will begin to take on a very bushy appearance. Hairs on the forward part of the head need not be full length as the head will have to be trimmed eventually. The drawing below shows how to obtain two spinnings from one length of hairs.

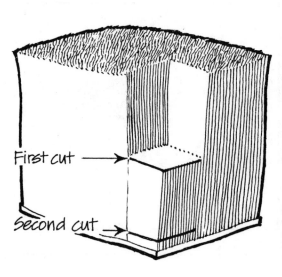

First cut →

Second cut →

Spin the deer hair up to the eye, whip finish and varnish.

Very carefully start to trim the deer hair using sharp fly-tying scissors. The hair points forming the first spinning can be left to slope back over the body.

Finished head shape

# Tying a Jersey Herd

Place a long-shank № 6-10 hook in the vice and run the tying silk down to the bend. Tie in a length of wool, flat gold tinsel and a bunch of peacock herl.

Take the silk back to a point short of the eye. Wind the wool towards the hanging silk, building up a cigar-shaped body in the process. Tie down the wool and trim off any excess. The gold tinsel is now wound over the wool body, tied down and trimmed.

Select a hot orange cock hackle and wind on in front of the body.

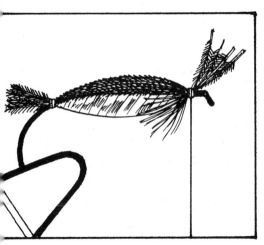

Bring the peacock herls over the body and hackle and tie them down, but do not trim away the excess herl.

Take the tying silk close to the eye and wind the excess herl around the shank to form a head.

Finish off in the usual manner.

# Tying a Matuka lure

Place a long-shanked N°6-10 hook in the vice. Build up a body, which in most matuka patterns is made of chenille, and leave the rib (oval tinsel) hanging, ready for use.

Select a large hen hackle and pull most of the fibres off on one side of the quill.

Place the prepared hackle on top of the body to see if it fits — the hackle should extend over the hook bend by about one-third of the body length. Take two or three turns of silk around the base of the quill to trap the hackle in position.

Very carefully start to wind the rib back through the hackle, adjusting the hackle fibres in the process. Tie down the rib, turn the fly over and tie in a beard hackle. Build up a head with the tying silk, whip finish and coat with black varnish.

# Tying a Dog Nobbler

Put a long-shanked hook in the vice and take the tying silk to the bend of the hook.

Select a generous bunch of fibres from a marabou plume and tie in. Cut a length of chenille, tie it down next to the marabou and run the silk back to a point about 5mm short of the eye.

Wind the chenille along the hook shank to form a body, and tie down. Trim off any excess chenille and form a whip finish.

Smear a layer of waterproof glue over the shank of the hook between the body and the eye and squeeze on a non-toxic split shot. Final tightening with a gentle squeeze from a pair of pliers will guarantee a firm hold. Finally, give the shot a coat of black varnish.

# Tying a Shrimp

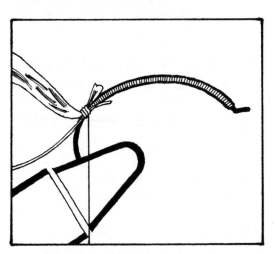

A curved-shank hook will be required to tie this very effective imitation. The 'caddis' hooks made by Partridge are ideal in sizes 16-10.

Take the silk from the eye to a point well around the bend and tie in a length of oval gold tinsel and a length of raffine or clear polythene.

Wax the hanging tying silk and dub with seal's fur. Use a mixture of 90% cream or pale orange and 10% fluorescent red. Wind the dubbed silk to a point just short of the eye.

Pull the raffine or polythene completely over the top of the body, and tie it down.

If raffine is being used it must be dampened before doing this.

Now bring the ribbing, in neat spirals, over and along the body, and tie it down. Trim off the excess body shell material and ribbing and build up a neat head. Whip finish, and apply a coat of clear varnish over the head and shell back.

Tying silk colours for this pattern can be cream, orange, yellow or red.

Using a dubbing needle, tease out strands of the body material to give a more life-like appearance.

This pattern can be tied to a standard-shank sproat hook, but in so doing ensure that the curved body shape is retained, by taking the dressing well around the hook bend.

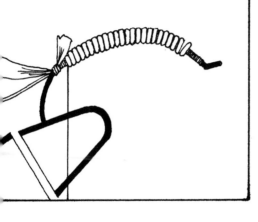

As this little creation is best fished well down in the water it is a good policy to add weight by running a length of lead wire along the shank of the hook before winding on the body.

# Tying a Daddy-long-legs

Clamp a long-shanked size 10 hook in the vice and run well-waxed tying silk from the eye to the bend. Tie in a length of raffia or raffine and bring the silk back about two-thirds of the way along the shank. Follow this with the body material, tie down and trim away any excess.

Cut a slip of fibres from a cock pheasant tail feather (the longer the better) and, one by one, separate them and tie a simple knot in the middle. Put these aside on a sheet of white paper or foam.

Turn the hook over in the vice. Select at least six fibres, more if you like, and hold them together between finger and thumb. Rotate them a few times to give a bedraggled look and tie them immediately in front of the body.

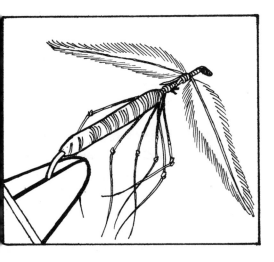

Select two white or honey colour cock hackles and prepare them as you would for tying a spent dry fly. Whip them to the hook so that they point outwards and slightly back.

Variation

The hackle is then tied, using a natural red cock hackle, in exactly the same way as the hackle on a spent dry fly. Form a whip finish and coat the head with clear varnish.

Variation

# Tying a sedge (caddis) fly

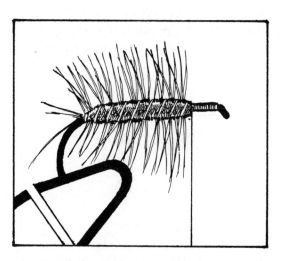

This is another pattern with many variations. Species of the natural insect are numerous and vary in size from the huge great red sedge or murragh, to the smaller sedges, such as silverhorns and yellow sedge

A good impressionistic pattern can be made by tying a palmered body, as described earlier.

After the body is complete lay a matching pair of wing slips, taken from a mottled turkey tail feather or a hen pheasant wing feather, over the hackle, and tie down to lie low along the body. Immediately in front of the wings, tie in a good quality cock hackle.

This type of dressing provides enough buoyancy, when treated with floatant, to be dragged across the water surface, giving a life-like, scuttling impression of the natural insect.

# Storing materials

Fly-tying materials should be stored in a case or cabinet. Portable cases are available on the market, at a reasonable cost. A cabinet, however, will probably have to be specially made. My cabinet is a mahogany creation and was made during the Georgian period. Whether it was originally intended to hold fly-tying materials I do not know, but it certainly does the job well, and is a pleasure to use.

Furs, feathers and floss suffer the depredations of moths if precautions are not taken. A small container housing a napthalene ball will keep these pests away.

Portable fly-tying case

Cabinet

Napthalene container